Were You There?

Were You There?

Lenten Reflections on the Spirituals

LUKE A. POWERY

WITHDRAWN

WJK WESTMINSTER
JOHN KNOX PRESS
LOUISVILLE · KENTUCKY

First edition
Published by Westminster John Knox Press
Louisville, Kentucky

19 20 21 22 23 24 25 26 27 28—10 9 8 7 6 5 4 3 2 1

Book design by Sharon Adams
Cover design by designpointinc.com
Cover illustration: Velvet Spirit, *1994 (oil on canvas), Hoyes, Bernard Stanley*
(contemporary artist) / Private Collection / Bridgeman Images

Library of Congress Cataloging-in-Publication Data is on file at the Library of Congress, Washington, DC.

ISBN-13: 9780664260309

For
Emittie V. Powery (Mom)
Dorothy A. Berlin (Aunt Dor)
Leitha E. Bent (Aunt Leitha)
Ura A. Russell (Aunt Ura)

*These are the St. Elizabeth sister-saints who laughed,
even in their suffering.*

Contents

Week Three

Week Four

Week Five

Week Six

Holy Week

Preface

There is no lack of pain and suffering in the world. Look around. Read the newspaper. Click on the Internet. Scroll Facebook or read a tweet. Suffering is always present like the paparazzi. It seems to stalk its human prey. Suffering is a part of the broken, sin-sick world. And if there is a theo-musical genre that reminds us of this, it is the Spirituals. They are musical memorabilia created on the anvil of misery by enslaved Blacks. They are sorrow songs. They are suffering songs. However, to sing can be a sting to the reality of suffering. It can be a sign of hope and the presence of God in the midst of agony. This is why they are called the "Spirituals" because they are the Spirit's song and the Spirit will not be stopped and will blow through every season of life, even liturgical seasons like Lent.

This little book of daily meditations on the Spirituals for the Christian season of Lent merges these two worlds (cultural-historical Black music with the church calendar) in order to help the reader travel the forty days of the Lenten wilderness with courage and honesty. Lent is a season of penitential reflection and repentance on the path toward the hope of Easter. That path walks in a dry desert where there is no water. The enslaved lived in their own inhumane wilderness for years, yet still sang songs of hope. From these cultural wells, we still drink.

These honest musical expressions—the Spirituals—in a Lenten mode quench our spiritual thirst and make up the main text of each day followed by a brief reflection. There are options given for daily Scripture readings as well as a portion of Scripture included. Each day closes with a short prayer. My prayer is that even in the laments, the reader will see the tiny sprout of hope springing from the page.

Furthermore, no book is an island. There have been so many influences, experiences, and people who have made this book possible. As I reflect on this, my heart is a eucharist, full of thanksgiving to God and every person who has encouraged me, especially in this work on the Spirituals. None of us are self-created, so hearty thanks goes to the great cloud of witnesses, seen and unseen: Duke University Chapel staff and community, Duke Divinity School colleagues, and all of the institutions and churches that have been patient enough to allow me to share my passion for the Spirituals. Jack Adams, my excellent administrative assistant at the Chapel, administered my schedule so I can minister through these pages. Tim Buskey, my research assistant for this project, was fabulous, and without him, there would only be a blank page. Bob Ratcliff, executive editor at Westminster John Knox Press, has been undying in his support of my work; he has made this book even better!

Beyond these, I thank God for my nuclear family—my wife, Gail, and children, Moriah and Zachary; I may have caused them much lament during this book process, but they fill me with hope. Speaking of family, this book is dedicated to some of the sweetest women I have known throughout my life—my mother and three of her sisters. They all were acquainted with grief, sorrow, and suffering yet their lives vibrated with laughing hope.

For many, life is a Lent. But I pray that this small offering would bring you into God's presence to know that Jesus is right there with you in your suffering and pain. He is there, a God with us, even with his scars of cruciform salvation. See his hands. See his feet. See the mingled blood and love flow down from his crowned head. Walk to him. Run to him. He's calling you. He's calling you there. Go there, to the cross where they crucified my Lord. Go there, so when someone asks you, "Were you there?" you can say, "Yes." This will change your life, because in Christ's dying, we discover what it means to live.

Luke A. Powery

Week One

Day 1 (Ash Wednesday)

Joel 2:1–2, 12–17 or Isaiah 58:1–12; Psalm 51:1–17;
Matthew 6:1–6, 16; 2 Corinthians 5:20b—6:10

Didn't My Lord Deliver Daniel?

Refrain:
Didn't my Lord deliver Daniel
Deliver Daniel, deliver Daniel
Didn't my Lord deliver Daniel
An' why not-a every man.

He delivered Daniel f'om de lion's den
Jonah f'om de belly of de whale
An' de Hebrew chillun f'om de fiery furnace
An' why not every man.

De moon run down in a purple stream,
De sun forbear to shine
An' every star disappear,
King Jesus shall-a be mine.

De win' blows eas' an' de win' blows wes'
It blows like de judg-a-ment day,

3

An' ev'ry po' sinner dat never did pray'll,
Be glad to pray dat day
Deliver Daniel, deliver Daniel

I set my foot on de Gospel ship,
An' de ship begin to sail,
It landed me over on Canaan's shore
An' I'll never come back no mo'.
—*The Books of American Negro Spirituals**

At the beginning of this season of Lent, on this Ash Wednesday, we are reminded that we are dust and to dust we will return. We are reminded of human fragility and failure. We are reminded that we are human, *humus*, from the soil of the earth. Though we are God's creation, we are dingy and dirty and dusty and are often in need of cleansing. *We* are. Not someone else, but we are. I am in need. I need deliverance. I need freedom. Didn't my Lord deliver Daniel f'om de lion's den? Didn't my Lord deliver Jonah f'om de belly of de whale and de Hebrew chillun f'om de fiery furnace? So why not every man?

The spiritual basically raises the question, "So why not me? I'm in need of deliverance, maybe not from a lion's den or the belly of a whale or a fiery furnace, but I'm trapped." Wherever you might be or whatever it might be, God's mighty acts throughout history reveal the liberating power of God. What God did for Daniel, Jonah, the Hebrew children, and so many others, God will do for you this Lent. God will deliver you. Can't you see it coming?

*James Weldon Johnson and J. Rosamond Johnson, eds., *The Books of American Negro Spirituals* (New York: Viking Press, 1940), 148–51.

Between the vestibule and the altar
    let the priests, the ministers of the LORD, weep.
Let them say, "Spare your people, O LORD,
    and do not make your heritage a mockery,
    a byword among the nations.
Why should it be said among the peoples,
    'Where is their God?'"

                      (Joel 2:17)

Prayer for the Day
Dear God, deliver me, even from myself.

Day 2 (Thursday)

Exodus 5:10–23; Psalm 91:1–2, 9–16; Acts 7:30–34

Many Thousand Gone

No more auction block for me, No more, No more,
No more auction block for me, Many thousand gone.

No more peck o' corn for me, No more, No more,
No more peck o' corn for me, Many thousand gone.

No more driver's lash for me, No more, No more,
No more driver's lash for me, Many thousand gone.

No more pint o' salt for me, No more, No more,
No more pint o' salt for me, Many thousand gone.

No more hundred lash for me, No more, No more,
No more hundred lash for me, Many thousand gone.

No more mistress' call for me, No more, No more,
No more mistress' call for me, Many thousand gone.
—*Songs of Zion**

**Songs of Zion: Supplemental Resources 12* (Nashville: Abingdon Press, 1981), 137.

As this spiritual emphasizes there are "many thousand gone." It speaks to the true and harsh reality of many who suffered and died under the brutal force of human slavery. If we can't face the truth of the past, we will not be able to move forward into a brighter future. This spiritual tells the truth of the inhumane system of slavery, and if you can't tell the truth during Lent, when can you? It is true—the auction blocks, the peck o' corn, the driver's lash, the hundred lash, the pint o' salt, the mistress' call. And through all the pain and toil and danger, many thousand were gone. They died and are no more. This is pure lament and a declaration that "enough is enough."

Maybe you are at that point of "enough is enough" and you are saying "no more" over and over again, just like this spiritual. No more suffering. No more pain. No more injustice. No more death. What have you had enough of? Tell the truth to yourself and others. "No more" is a linguistic form of resistance to death. If you don't want to be gone like the many thousand, then today declare, "no more." Tell God what it is and what you want more of. Tell the truth, because although it may make you sick at first to say it, it will eventually set you free!

So the taskmasters and the supervisors of the people went out and said to the people, "Thus says Pharaoh, 'I will not give you straw. Go and get straw yourselves, wherever you can find it; but your work will not be lessened in the least.'" So the people scattered throughout the land of Egypt, to gather stubble for straw. The taskmasters were urgent, saying, "Complete your work, the same daily assignment as when you were given straw." And the supervisors of the Israelites, whom Pharaoh's taskmasters had set over them, were beaten, and were asked, "Why did you not finish the required quantity of bricks yesterday and today, as you did before?"

(Exod. 5:10–14)

Prayer for the Day

Lord, I can't take it anymore. You know what it is and today, I say with courage, "No more, no more."

Day 3 (Friday)

Exodus 6:1–13; Psalm 91:1–2, 9–16; Acts 7:35–42

Let God's Saints Come In

Come down, angel, and trouble the water,
Come down, angel, and trouble the water,
Come down, angel, and trouble the water,
And let God's saints come in.

Canaan land is the land for me,
And let God's saints come in.
Canaan land is the land for me,
And let God's saints come in.

There was a wicked man,
He kept them children in Egypt land.

God did say to Moses one day,
Say, Moses go to Egypt land,

And tell him to let my people go.
And Pharaoh would not let 'em go.

God did go to Moses' house,
And God did tell him who he was,

> God and Moses walked and talked,
> And God did show him who he was.
> —*Slave Songs of the United States**

Lent is a time of reflection, penitence, repentance, and even spiritual wandering or wondering. It is a journey accompanied by ashes. Often, it seems to put focus on individuals and our own spiritual lives and need for growth. What this spiritual does, however, is call us out of ourselves to a larger vision. It not only stresses the "children in Egypt land" and "my people," thus, the children of Israel who were in bondage in Egypt, but it emphasizes "God's saints." What this does is push us toward a communal sensibility and recognition of the community of faith who are also on this same journey with us.

Canaan land may be "the land for me," but there's a clear desire to be joined by others by declaring "and let God's saints come in." This spiritual calls us to move beyond a selfish spirituality toward a selfless one, one that wants all of God's people to reach Canaan too, all of God's children to be delivered out of Egypt. It also suggests that the singer/speaker doesn't want to be alone but in community. The singer wants others to experience the freedom and joy of Canaan land. Let God's saints come in. It is a spirit of welcome and inclusion that is so often missing. This spiritual compels us toward "we" instead of "me."

Then the LORD said to Moses, "Now you shall see what I will do to Pharaoh: Indeed, by a mighty hand he

---

*William Francis Allen, Charles Pickard Ware, and Lucy McKim Garrison, *Slave Songs of the United States* (New York: A. Simpson & Co., 1867), 76.

will let them go; by a mighty hand he will drive them out of his land."

(Exod. 6:1)

Prayer for the Day

Come down, God, and trouble the water. Not just for me, but for all of God's saints. Free me toward inclusivity. Let the saints come into your promised land. Let them enter your joy and freedom, just as I have.

Day 4 (Saturday)

Psalm 91:1–2, 9–16; Ecclesiastes 3:1–8; John 12:27–36

Hold Your Light

What make ole Satan da follow me so?
Satan hain't nottin' at all for to do wid me.

(Run seeker.)
Hold your light,
(Sister Mary)
Hold your light,
(Seeker turn back,)
Hold your light on Canaan shore.

—Slave Songs, 10

In the Lenten wilderness, there is temptation, darkness, and doubt. The wilderness can get us weary and worn out. When tired and weak, Satan, the evil one, may follow us, seeking to devour us, turning us away from Jesus. It happened to Jesus when he was tempted. On the journey, there are ups and downs. It is dark, but there is also light.

The light is Jesus Christ. To "hold your light" as we travel means to hold on to Jesus, the Light of lights, for he will direct our paths and way forward. He will show us where to go. He will show us Canaan, the land flowing with milk and honey. Lent is never too dark for Christ to shine on our path. Even in the wilderness, there is a light that we can hold because this Light holds us. We can keep running and keep seeking and keep discerning the way as long as this light shines. Are you holding it as your guide, or are you holding something else?

> Jesus said to them, "The light is with you for a little longer. Walk while you have the light, so that the darkness may not overtake you. If you walk in the darkness, you do not know where you are going. While you have the light, believe in the light, so that you may become children of light."
>
> (John 12:35–36)

Prayer for the Day
Let this "little light of mine" shine but let the light of Jesus shine even brighter and lead me where I need to go.

Week Two

Day 1 (Monday)

Deuteronomy 26:1–11; Psalm 91:1–2, 9–16;
Romans 10:8b–13; Luke 4:1–13

O Brothers, Don't Get Weary

O brothers, don't get weary,
O brothers, don't get weary,
O brothers, don't get weary,
We're waiting for the Lord.

We'll land on Canaan's shore,
We'll land on Canaan's shore,
When we land on Canaan's shore,
We'll meet forever more.
—*Slave Songs*, 95

If we are honest with ourselves, there are days when we get weary, even from well-doing. This is because we are human. Just because we may be Christians doesn't mean we are superhuman. Actually, to be a Christian suggests that we are anointed ones ("Christ" means "anointed one"); thus we receive power for living and dying. It means we are empowered. It means we have to wait on the Lord.

Sometimes waiting for the Lord means waiting a very long time. This is why the spiritual singer encourages the listener, "Don't get weary." She knew this is the human way—to get weary while waiting. At the same time, the singer knew that waiting for the Lord was worth it, which is why she urges us not to get weary and wear out because the wait is worth it. Why? Because we will "land on Canaan's shore." We will land. No ifs, ands, or buts. We will. This singer knows something about God that we may not always believe—it's worth the wait. Even if you question this spiritual, remember what the prophet Isaiah proclaims, "those who wait for the LORD shall renew their strength; . . . they shall run and not be weary, they shall walk and not faint" (40:31). The saints of old possessed a dogged faith in God. I hope you discover this faith also, for we will land, not just on Canaan's shore, but wherever God wants us to be in the end. Don't get weary. Get wonder at what's next on the journey.

> So the LORD brought us out of Egypt with a mighty hand and an outstretched arm, with a terrifying display of power, and with signs and wonders; and he brought us into this place and gave us this land, a land flowing with milk and honey.
>
> (Deut. 26:8–9)

Prayer for the Day

I wait on you, Lord. Wash away any sense of weariness and instill in me a sense of wonder and awe at your presence and power. Take me to the shore of your salvation so I can be safe forevermore.

Day 2 (Tuesday)

1 Chronicles 21:1–17; Psalm 17; 1 John 2:1–6

No Hiding Place

Refrain:
There's no hiding place down here,
There's no hiding place down here,

Went to the rocks for to hide my face,
Rocks cried out, "No hiding place,"
There's no hiding place down here.

Boatman, boatman, row one side,
Can't get to heav'n 'gainst wind and tide.
There's no hiding place down here.

Sinner man, sinner man, better repent,
God's going to call you to judgment.
There's no hiding place down here.
　　　*—Folk Songs of the American Negro**

---

*Frederick Jerome Work and John Wesley Work, *Folk Songs of the American Negro* (Nashville: Work Bros. & Hart Co., 1907), 30.

There's the oft-quoted phrase, "You can run, but you can't hide." It is so true, especially when it comes to God. We hustle to hide who we are, thinking that God won't know, but God has known us since we were in our mother's wombs. Apart from God, we may attempt to hide our true selves from others—our friends, colleagues, family members. We don't want them to know us, fully or deeply, because we may think there are things in our lives that may bring shame and we don't want them to change their image of us. We may attempt to hide our face or our souls. And perhaps we are good at this. We may even try to hide our true selves from ourselves, which may seem odd, but we may do that by overlooking what is inside of us. We run and sprint throughout the day, never slowing down, because we are afraid of what we might see when we watch ourselves pass by before our eyes.

The spiritual for the day encourages us not to hide from God. It would be pointless anyway because as is repeated over and over, "there's no hiding place down here." We can't hide behind rocks or row to the other side of a shore. We can't run away from God. God is always there. God is here, even as you are reading this. Today, stop hiding, unless you hide in the presence of Almighty God.

> Guard me as the apple of the eye;
>   hide me in the shadow of your wings,
> from the wicked who despoil me,
>   my deadly enemies who surround me.
>   (Ps. 17:8–9)

Prayer for the Day
Hide me, O God, in the shadow of your wings. Know me, yet still love me.

Day 3 (Wednesday)

Psalm 17; Zechariah 3:1–10; 2 Peter 2:4–21

My Way's Cloudy

O bretheren my way,
My way's cloudy, my way,
Go sen' a dem angels down.
O, bretheren, my way,
My way's cloudy, my way;
Go sen' a dem angels down.

Dere's fire in de eas' an' fire in de wes'
Sen' dem angels down,
Dere's fire among dem Methodis'
Oh, sen' a dem angels down.

Old Satan is mad an' I'm so glad,
Sen' dem angels down,
He missed de soul he thought he had
Oh, sen'a dem angels down.

—The Books of American
Negro Spirituals, 92–93

If you were to look at a map of the world, you might see little figures of light sparkling from the map. Those lights signify the parts of the world that are burning. Burning because it's on fire due to civil unrest, governmental corruption, lack of clean water, poor education, and other social ills. If we are honest, the world is on fire. "Dere's fire in de eas' an' fire in de wes'." Dere's fire all over the land. To be sure, it's not only the civic realm but also the religious context that has its own struggles. This spiritual doesn't let the church off the hook either! "Dere's fire among dem Methodis'," and we could add any other denomination to this list! The church is in splinters, though we see pockets of hope of the kingdom of God. Yet, there are fires burning that could devour the church as we know it. All of these fires produce a lot of smoke and can make your way cloudy.

You may not see clearly right now because "my way's cloudy, my way." The larger global and local setting impact us personally. What's happening "out there" can influence "in here," in our hearts and minds. It can muddy the waters and cloud our way forward, thus we may not see straight and know exactly where to go. Call on God to send his angels down with their holy light to rescue you and to make your way clearer. Trust that "old Satan" won't catch your soul and set it on fire to burn you up. May the only fire that is lit in your heart be the fire of the Holy Spirit. Send that fire, Lord, today on my way, my way, my way.

> Then he showed me the high priest Joshua standing before the angel of the LORD, and Satan standing at his right hand to accuse him. And the LORD said to Satan,

"The LORD rebuke you, O Satan! The LORD who has chosen Jerusalem rebuke you!"

(Zech. 3:1–2a)

Prayer for the Day

Lord, my way is so cloudy right now. Blow on it to clear the clouds of doubt away and make my soul happy.

Day 4 (Thursday)

Psalm 17; Job 1:1–22; Luke 21:34–22:6

Sometimes I Feel like a Motherless Chile

Sometimes I feel like a motherless chile,
Sometimes I feel like a motherless chile,
Sometimes I feel like a motherless chile,
A long ways from home,
A long ways from home.
Then I get down on my knees an' pray,
Get down on my knees an' pray.

Sometimes I feel like I'm almos' gone,
Sometimes I feel like I'm almos' gone,
Sometimes I feel like I'm almos' gone,
A long ways from home,
A long ways from home.
Then I get down on my knees an' pray,
Get down on my knees an' pray.
—*Songs of Zion*, 83

You don't have to be a child to feel motherless or "a long ways from home." There are those who are literally homeless and motherless, but there are those beyond these who are dislocated and lost. To journey during Lent is to acknowledge this reality—that "sometimes I feel like I'm almos' gone." Fed up. Done. Enough. Can't take anymore. Almos' gone. By yourself on the road of life and home is nowhere in sight. This is a common human experience, if we are honest. Be honest today about yourself, about others, about the world. Sometimes we all feel like motherless children. The question, however, is how do we respond? When we are lonely and lost and disconnected from family or all that is familiar, what do we do? What do you do?

The spiritual writer points us in a good direction. "I get down on my knees an' pray." In other words, I turn to God. I turn to God because God is our eternal home, our mother and father. If we try other approaches, they may not be the best for us. Some will turn to drugs, sex, money, or other fleeting activities. When we are lost, we can only be found by God and in God. Be found in God today and get down on your knees and pray.

While he was still speaking, another came and said, "Your sons and daughters were eating and drinking wine in their eldest brother's house, and suddenly a great wind came across the desert, struck the four corners of the house, and it fell on the young people, and they are dead; I alone have escaped to tell you." Then Job arose, tore his robe, shaved his head, and fell on the ground and worshiped. He said, "Naked I came from my mother's womb, and naked shall I return there; the Lord gave, and the Lord has taken away; blessed be the name of the Lord." In all this Job did not sin or charge God with wrongdoing.

(Job 1:18–22)

Prayer for the Day

I get down on my knees and pray and say, "I'm a long ways from home" but lead me back home to You.

Day 5 (Friday)

Genesis 13:1–7, 14–18; Psalm 27; Philippians 3:2–12

Didn't Old Pharaoh Get Los'?

Isaac a-ransom
While he lay upon an altar bound;
Moses an infant cast away,
By Pharaoh's daughter found.

Refrain:
Didn't old Pharaoh los', get los', get los'
Didn't old Pharaoh get los'
In de Red Sea, True believer
O, didn't old Pharaoh los', get los', get los'
Didn't old Pharaoh get los'
In de Red Sea.

Joseph by his false brethren sold,
God raised above them all
To Hannah's child the Lord foretold
How Eli's house shall fall

27

De Lord said unto Moses—
"Go unto Pharaoh now,
For I have hardened Pharaoh's heart,
To me he will not bow"

Den Moses an' Aaron,
To Pharaoh did go,
"Thus says de God of Israel,
Let my people go."

Old Pharaoh said, "Who is de Lord
Dat I should him obey?"
"His name it is Jehovah.
For he hears his people pray."

Hark! Hear de children murmur,
Dey cry aloud for bread,
Down came de hidden manna,
De hungry soldiers fed.

Den Moses numbered Israel,
Through all de land abroad,
Sayin', "Children, do not murmur,
But hear de word of God."

Den Moses said to Israel,
As dey stood along de Shore,
"Yo' enemies you see today,
You'll never see no more."

Den down came raging Pharaoh,
Dat you may plainly see,
Old Pharaoh an' his host
Got los' in de Red Sea.

Den men an' women an' children
To Moses dey did flock;

Dey cried aloud for water,
An' Moses smote de rock.

An' de Lord spoke to Moses,
From Sinai's smoking top,
Sayin', "Moses lead de people,
Till I shall bid you stop."
—*Books of American Negro
Spirituals*, 60–61

This is a spiritual of great faith and a testimony of triumph. Repeatedly in the refrain, we are told that old Pharaoh got los' in the Red Sea, alluding to when the children of Israel escaped out of Egypt led by Moses. It is a story of deliverance. A story of triumph by the hand of God. But it's not just this biblical story. There are other testimonies of triumph in the Bible. Isaac when he lay on the altar to be sacrificed by his father Abraham but was spared. Moses, as an infant, when he was found in the water by Pharaoh's daughter and saved. Joseph and Hannah's child, too. There are many who have experienced the faithfulness of God. Not just one, but many. Not just those in the Scriptures, but you, too.

How has God delivered you? What is your story? What is your testimony of how you have seen and heard the living God at work in your own life? God worked then and still works today. Let it be known to others of how God has moved in your life. Tell the story. Testify! That way, others will know that God is the same, yesterday, today, and forever.

The LORD is my light and my salvation; whom shall I fear? The LORD is the stronghold of my life; of whom shall I be afraid?

(Ps. 27:1)

Prayer for the Day

Dear delivering God, open up my stammering tongue to let the world know how you brought me out of Egypt and through the Red Sea to a safe land. Fill my heart with a testimony of triumph.

Day 6 (Saturday)

Psalm 20; Habakkuk 3:2–15; Luke 18:31–34

Heaven Bell A-Ring

My Lord, my Lord, what shall I do?
And a heav'n bell a-ring and praise God.

Timmy, Timmy, orphan boy.
Robert, Robert, orphan child.

What shall I do for a hiding place?
And a heav'n, &c.
I run to de sea, but de sea run dry.
I run to de gate, but de gate shut fast.
No hiding place for sinner dere.

Say you when you get to heaven say you 'member me.
Remember me, poor fallen soul.
Say when you get to heaven say your work shall prove.
Your righteous Lord shall prove 'em well.

Your righteous Lord shall find you out.
He cast out none dat come by faith.

You look to de Lord wid a tender heart.
I wonder where poor Monday dere.

For I am gone and sent to hell.
We must harkee what de worldy say.
Say Christmas come but once a year.
Say Sunday come but once a week.
　　　　　　　　　—*Slave Songs*, 27

We can be so heavenly minded that we're no earthly good. But the Spirituals help us keep in mind heaven, God's future, without neglecting the earth. This song speaks of orphan boys, orphan children, and days of the week. There's a sense of being lost and running all over the place—to the sea, to the gate, in order to somehow hide. And during this rigmarole of restlessness, heaven bell a-ring. The bell tolls and time is up. We can't stop the bells from ringing and they toll for all of us, eventually.

Currently, you may find yourself in a season of restlessness and ask, "What shall I do?" You've tried to figure out everything on your own but you can't run from God. You can't run from when your time on earth is done. The bells will ring. What shall you do? What shall you do today? Through it all, do what the spiritual says—"praise God" for whether we live or die, we are the Lord's (Rom. 14:8).

O LORD, I have heard of your renown,
　　and I stand in awe, O LORD, of your work.
In our own time revive it;
　　in our own time make it known;
　　in wrath may you remember mercy.

God came from Teman,
the Holy One from Mount Paran.
His glory covered the heavens,
And the earth was full of his praise.
(Hab. 3:1–3)

Prayer for the Day
What shall I do? I will praise You today.

Week Three

Day 1 (Monday)

Psalm 27; Psalm 118:26–29; Matthew 23:37–39

Oh, Mary, Don't You Weep, Don't You Mourn

Oh Mary, don't you weep, don't you mourn,
Oh Mary, don't you weep, don't you mourn;
Pharaoh's army got drownded,
Oh Mary, don't you weep.

Some of these mornings bright and fair,
Take my wings and cleave the air.
Pharaoh's army got drownded,
Oh Mary, don't you weep

When I get to Heaven goin' to sing and shout,
Nobody there for to turn me out.
Pharaoh's army got drownded,
Oh Mary, don't you weep

When I get to Heaven goin' to put on my shoes,
Run about Glory and tell all the news.
Pharaoh's army got drownded,
Oh Mary, don't you weep
—Songs of Zion, 153

"O Mary, don't you weep." This spiritual emphasizes this—the fact that Mary is weeping when Jesus died (John 20) but she's encouraged not to weep. Weeping is a part of the Christian life. There is sorrow, grief, and suffering. There are crosses to bear. Some folks may want to avoid this and see it as antithetical to faith but it's not. Even "Jesus wept" (John 11:35 KJV). There may be times you've wept too—over the death of a loved one, a loss of some kind, a disappointment. There's nothing wrong with this because it just means you are human before God. But also remember that your tears that flow may be a sign of the waters of your baptism. Your weeping may be an overflowing of the Spirit in your life, too. It may indicate how much you care and how much you love something or someone. At the same time, we should be careful to not allow weeping to whip us around in life and taint our memory for what we remember matters. What we remember and who we remember are key.

In this spiritual, remembering that "Pharaoh's army got drownded" is critical. It's less about what happened to Pharaoh and more about remembering what God can do to deliver you and anyone else. It's remembering that God is faithful and will save you from hard times. We may have to constantly be reminded not to weep and not to mourn because our memory is faulty. We need the community of faith to help us recall the past and to remember our future. This spiritual created out of an enslaved community helps us remember that one day we will "run about Glory" and "take my wings" and fly and that God is consistent—what God did back then, God can do now. Be encouraged. Don't you weep. And remember, weeping may endure for the night, but joy comes in the morning (Ps. 30:5)!

"Jerusalem, Jerusalem, the city that kills the prophets and stones those who are sent to it! How often have I desired to gather your children together as a hen gathers her brood under her wings, and you were not willing! See, your house is left to you, desolate. For I tell you, you will not see me again until you say, 'Blessed is the one who comes in the name of the Lord.'"

(Matt. 23:37–39)

Prayer for the Day

Lord, you are acquainted with grief and sorrow. You know what weeping is because you've done it too. Help us to embrace our weeping as a part of our spirituality but also teach us that our weeping is not the final word. Help us to remember that you still deliver.

Day 2 (Tuesday)

Genesis 15:1–12, 17–18; Psalm 27; Luke 13:31–35
or Luke 9:28–36; Philippians 3:17–4:1

Kum Ba Yah, My Lord

Kum ba yah, my Lord, Kum ba yah,
Kum ba yah, my Lord, Kum ba yah,
Kum ba yah, my Lord, Kum ba yah,
Oh, Lord, Kum ba yah.

Someone's cryin', Lord, Kum ba yah,
Someone's cryin', Lord, Kum ba yah,
Someone's cryin', Lord, Kum ba yah,
Oh, Lord, Kum ba yah.

Someone's singin', Lord, Kum ba yah,
Someone's singin', Lord, Kum ba yah,
Someone's singin', Lord, Kum ba yah,
Oh, Lord, Kum ba yah.

Someone's prayin', Lord, Kum ba yah,
Someone's prayin', Lord, Kum ba yah,
Someone's prayin', Lord, Kum ba yah,
Oh, Lord, Kum ba yah.

Someone needs you, Lord, Kum ba yah,
Someone needs you, Lord, Kum ba yah,
Someone needs you, Lord, Kum ba yah,
Oh, Lord, Kum ba yah.
                    —*Songs of Zion*, 139

Regardless of where one finds themselves on the Lenten journey, this spiritual reveals a yearning heart that resonates with many who find themselves in a wilderness. That heart makes a repetitive plea: "Kum ba yah, my Lord," translated, "Come by here, my Lord." Come by here. It is a prayer for the presence of God wherever one might find oneself. If one is crying or singing or praying, what is obvious is that "someone needs you, Lord." This is true every day of the year. Someone needs God, right now.

You might need God right now, today, regardless of your situation. Things may be fine with you. You could be singing up a storm full of joy, but this doesn't neglect the need to pray, "Kum ba yah, my Lord," nor your need of God in your life. This repeating line challenges us to make these words our words repeatedly. It suggests our vast need for the Presence. Come by here, my Lord. It would be a sad pilgrimage without God. It would be lonely but the spiritual reveals a faith that, in asking, believes that the Lord will come by here, will come by you, today. Underneath these words of prayer is the reminder that when we pray this, God will come because God is a God who is with us (Matt. 1:23). Here. There. And everywhere. With you. Today. Now.

As the sun was going down, a deep sleep fell upon Abram, and a deep and terrifying darkness descended upon him. . . . When the sun had gone down and it was dark, a smoking fire pot and a flaming torch passed between these pieces. On that day the LORD made a covenant with Abram, saying, "To your descendants I give this land, from the river of Egypt to the great river, the river Euphrates."

(Gen. 15:12, 17–18)

Prayer for the Day

Kum ba yah, my Lord. Come by here, my Lord, even now.

Day 3 (Wednesday)

Exodus 33:1–6; Psalm 105:1–15 [16–41], 42;
Romans 4:1–12

Give Up the World

De sun give a light in de heaven all round,
De sun give a light in de heaven all round,
De sun give a light in de heaven all round,
Why don't you give up de world?

My brudder, don't you give up de world?
My brudder, don't you give up de world?
My brudder, don't you give up de world?
We must leave de world behind.
—*Slave Songs*, 37

Lent is often a time when people give up something they really love, like chocolate or Facebook. This giving up is a kind of fasting that hopefully allows people to be more open to Jesus; thus, by giving up, one gains. Chocolate or Facebook is part of our worldly existence, and the giving up is an attempt, even if only for forty days, to shed some of the world from our spiritual walk. There's some tension here because as we know, "God so loved the world" (John

3:16). But at the same time, there are things in the world and of the world that can hinder our walk with Christ.

Lent provides an opportunity to reflect on "Why don't you give up de world?" What should you give up this season that is holding you up in your faith journey? What is getting in the way, "my brudder," my sister? Only you know what that is. Be honest today and ask yourself, "What do I need to give up for Jesus?"

> The LORD said to Moses, "Go, leave this place, you and the people whom you have brought up out of the land of Egypt, and go to the land of which I swore to Abraham, Isaac, and Jacob, saying, "To your descendants I will give it."
>
> (Exod. 33:1)

Prayer for the Day
I give up myself to you. I give as you have given.

Day 4 (Thursday)

Numbers 14:10b–24; Psalm 105:1–15 [16–41], 42;
1 Corinthians 10:1–13

Do, Lord, Remember Me

Do, Lord, do, Lord, Lord, remember me,
Do, Lord, do, Lord, Lord, remember me,
Do, Lord, do, Lord, Lord, remember me,
Do, Lord, remember me.

When I'm in trouble, Lord, remember me.
When I'm in trouble, Lord, remember me.
When I'm in trouble, Lord, remember me.
Do, Lord, remember me.

When I'm dyin', Lord, remember me.
When I'm dyin', Lord, remember me.
When I'm dyin', Lord, remember me.
Do, Lord, remember me.

When this world's on fire, Lord, remember me.
When this world's on fire, Lord, remember me.
When this world's on fire, Lord, remember me.
Do, Lord, remember me.

—*Songs of Zion*, 119

Memory can be tricky. We lose our memory. Our memory can be fickle. It can be selective. We may even remember wrongly by deleting important details or adding details that never happened. In the Bible, Jesus tells his disciples to "do this in remembrance of me" when it comes to the Last Supper (Luke 22:19). There are certainly things we should remember and do as an act of remembrance. The Bible, in fact, is a book of memory. We remember the past and we remember the future. We remember what God in Christ has done for the world. But the life of faith is not all about what we remember or how we remember or our own memory. It is also about God's memory.

"Do, Lord, remember me." When I'm in trouble, dyin', or when this world's on fire, Lord, remember me. The Lord also is called to remember us, to not forget the holy covenant with his people, to be faithful to his stead-fast love. We need God to remember us because when God does this, God re-members us, puts us back together to make us whole, to assure us of divine presence. God's memory is faithful and never suffers from amnesia. We can count on it. Remember this!

> And now, therefore, let the power of the Lord be great in the way that you promised when you spoke, saying,

>> "The Lord is slow to anger,
>> and abounding in steadfast love,
>> forgiving iniquity and transgression,
>> but by no means clearing the guilty,
>> visiting the iniquity of the parents
>> upon the children
>> to the third and the fourth generation."

Forgive the iniquity of this people according to the greatness of your steadfast love, just as you have pardoned this people, from Egypt even until now.

(Num. 14:17–19)

Prayer for the Day

Jesus, remember me when you come into your kingdom.

Day 5 (Friday)

2 Chronicles 20:1–22; Psalm 105:1–15 [16–41], 42;
Luke 13:22–31

Somebody's Knocking at Your Door

Somebody's knocking at your door,
Somebody's knocking at your door,
O sinner, why don't you answer?
Somebody's knocking at your door.

Knocks like Jesus,
Somebody's knocking at your door.
Knocks like Jesus,
Somebody's knocking at your door.

Can't you hear him?
Somebody's knocking at your door.
Can't you hear him?
Somebody's knocking at your door.

Answer Jesus.
Somebody's knocking at your door.
Answer Jesus.
Somebody's knocking at your door.

Jesus calls you.
Somebody's knocking at your door.
Jesus calls you.
Somebody's knocking at your door.

Can't you trust Him?
Somebody's knocking at your door.
Can't you trust Him?
Somebody's knocking at your door.
—*Songs of Zion*, 154

Knock. Knock. Who's there? Jesus. Jesus, who? I hope this isn't your answer for why you don't answer the door, the door of your heart. Can't you hear him? "Behold, I stand at the door, and knock" (Rev. 3:20 KJV). What prevents you from answering the door? It could be many things. But one thing is certain—Jesus calls you. We aren't the only ones knocking at heaven's door. Jesus is knocking at ours! Are you ready to answer? "Can't you trust Him?" Opening that door may be the opening you've been waiting for. That opening is like an open, empty tomb, for your future that is wide open. When you open the door, Jesus will free you from all that is inside of you and has been holding you back from your freedom outside. Be free today and answer Jesus, who's knocking at your door. Open it and you will open your future.

Jesus went through one town and village after another, teaching as he made his way to Jerusalem. Someone asked him, "Lord, will only a few be saved?" He said to them, "Strive to enter through the narrow door; for many, I tell you, will try to enter and will not be able. When once the owner of the house has got up and shut the door, and you begin to stand outside and to knock

at the door, saying, 'Lord, open to us,' then in reply he
will say to you, 'I do not know where you come from.'
Then you will begin to say, 'We ate and drank with
you, and you taught in our streets.' But he will say, 'I
do not know where you come from; go away from me,
all you evildoers!' "

(Luke 13:22–27)

Prayer for the Day

*Keep knocking, Jesus, keep knocking. And give me the courage
to open the door of my heart to you.*

Day 6 (Saturday)

Psalm 63:1–8; Daniel 3:19–30; Revelation 2:8–11

My Father, How Long

My father, how long,
My father, how long,
My father, how long,
Poor sinner suffer here?

My mother, how long, . . .

And it won't be long,
And it won't be long,
And it won't be long,
Poor sinner suffer here

We'll soon be free,
We'll soon be free,
We'll soon be free,
De Lord will call us home.

We'll walk de miry road
We'll walk de miry road

We'll walk de miry road
Where pleasure never dies.

We'll walk de golden streets
We'll walk de golden streets
We'll walk de golden streets
Of de New Jerusalem

My brudders do sing
My brudders do sing
My brudders do sing
De praises of de Lord.

We'll fight for liberty
We'll fight for liberty
We'll fight for liberty
When de Lord will call us home.
—*Slave Songs*, 112

How long? It is an ancient question that still rings true today. How long? How long till justice rolls down? How long till school shootings cease? How long till the abuse of children ends? How long till we'll study war no more? How long till hatred and discrimination are over? How long till divides of any kind end? How long, Lord? My heavenly Father, how long? This question is not just a psalmist's question. It is a human question. There's nothing wrong with this question because it is honest and is a form of worship before God. We may ask this question, agonizing over how long suffering will be. The spiritual writer is clear that "it won't be long." The spiritual begins with the question but overwhelmingly consists of assurance that one day we'll be free, we'll walk de miry road, de golden streets, my brudders do sing, we'll fight for liberty. In other words, we will not always lament but we will praise. The whole story of your life is not lament but it is also praise. Both are true to the Christian life. Embrace both, knowing that sorrow and suffering will cease, and we'll approach a land "where pleasure never dies."

> My soul is satisfied as with a rich feast,
>   and my mouth praises you with joyful lips
> when I think of you on my bed,
>   and meditate on you in the watches of the night;
> for you have been my help,
>   and in the shadow of your wings I sing for joy.
> My soul clings to you;
>   your right hand upholds me.
>
> (Ps. 63:5–8)

Prayer for the Day
How long, O Lord? I hear you say, "Not long."

Week Four

Day 1 (Monday)

Psalm 63:1–8; Daniel 12:1–4; Revelation 3:1–6

We Will March through the Valley

We will march thro' the valley in peace,
We will march thro' the valley in peace;
If Jesus himself be our leader,
We will march thro' the valley in peace.

We will march, etc.
Behold I give myself away, and
We will march, etc.

We will march, etc.
This track I'll see and I'll pursue;
We will march, etc.

We will march, etc.
When I'm dead and buried in the cold silent tomb,
I don't want you to grieve for me.
                              —*Slave Songs*, 95

Life doesn't consist of only mountaintops, the high ecstatic moments. We all probably know this, just by living. Lent claims a wilderness journey. The psalmist claims a valley of the shadow of death (Ps. 23). It is the valley through which we also travel sometimes. And not only travel, "we will march." Marching is so much more intentional than mere walking. It takes determination to march, energy to march, focus to march, sheer will to march. When one marches, one has a destination in mind. The spiritual calls us not just to march but to march *through the valley*. It acknowledges the valley experience but it doesn't say we will die in the valley or faint in the valley but "we will march." Moreover, come what may in the valley, we will march "in peace." As we move forward, we will do so in peace but this peace is not of our own making.

The spiritual clarifies this just in case we thought we could march on our own and do so in peace. The singer makes it plain, "If Jesus himself be our leader, we will march through the valley in peace." Our peace in whatever circumstances we find ourselves in comes from Jesus, who is our peace (Eph. 2:14). Jesus has to lead in order for this to happen. "If Jesus . . ." suggests that at times we may travel, but Jesus isn't leading us to where we are going. Let Jesus lead you to where he wants you to go. *If* Jesus leads, you will find peace even if you march through a valley. Keep marching wherever Jesus leads.

"At that time Michael, the great prince, the protector of your people, shall arise. There shall be a time of anguish, such as has never occurred since nations first came into existence. But at that time your people shall be delivered, everyone who is found written in the book. Many of those who sleep in the dust of the earth shall awake, some to everlasting life, and some to shame and everlasting contempt. Those who are wise shall shine like the brightness of the sky, and those who lead many to righteousness, like the stars for ever and ever.

(Dan. 12:1–3)

Prayer for the Day

Lead me, Jesus, lead me. Even when I go through a valley, let me be consumed by your peace.

Day 2 (Tuesday)

Psalm 63:1–8; Isaiah 5:1–7; Luke 6:43–45

Michael Row the Boat Ashore

Michael row de boat ashore, Hallelujah!
Michael boat a gospel boat, Hallelujah!
I wonder where my mudder deh (there).
See my mudder on de rock gwine home.
On de rock gwine home in Jesus' name.
Michael boat a music boat.
Gabriel blow de trumpet horn.
O you mind your boastin' talk.
Boastin' talk will sink your soul.
Brudder, lend a helpin' hand.
Sister, help for trim dat boat.
Jordan stream is wide and deep.
Jesus stand on t' oder side.
I wonder if my maussa deh.
My fader gone to unknown land.
O de Lord he plant his garden deh.
He raise de fruit for you to eat.
He dat eat shall neber die.
When de riber overflow.
O poor sinner, how you land?

Riber run and darkness comin'.
Sinner row to save your soul.
                                    —*Slave Songs*, 31

All throughout the Christian life there is movement from one place to the next, from here to there, from exodus to the promised land, from crucifixion to the resurrection to the ascension, from down to up, from last to first, from lost to found. There is movement of one sort or another, for the life God has for us is not a stagnant one. Therefore, we must row. "Sinner row to save your soul." There are many rivers to cross to get to where God wants us to be. God wants us to keep on moving and this is how it has been throughout the generations. From Michael to mudder to Gabriel to sister to maussa to fader. The cloud of witnesses has been on the move to Jesus who "stand on t'oder side." Where are we going? To Jesus. We move to get closer to him. We aim for him. He's our telos, our goal, our end. He's our beginning, too. So keep rowing your boat till you reach him and reach the shore of salvation.

You may not always want to move. It may be hard. You may be stuck. Ask the winds of the Spirit to blow your boat onward so you can row your boat ashore.

> Let me sing for my beloved
>   my love-song concerning his vineyard:
> My beloved had a vineyard
>   on a very fertile hill.
> He dug it and cleared it of stones,
>   and planted it with choice vines;
> he built a watchtower in the midst of it,
>   and hewed out a wine vat in it;
> he expected it to yield grapes,
>   but it yielded wild grapes.

And now, inhabitants of Jerusalem
    and people of Judah,
judge between me
    and my vineyard.
What more was there to do for my vineyard
    that I have not done in it?
When I expected it to yield grapes,
    why did it yield wild grapes?

(Isa. 5:1–4)

Prayer for the Day

Michael rowed his boat ashore to you, Jesus. Let me do the same.

Day 3 (Wednesday)

Isaiah 55:1–9; Psalm 63:1–8;
1 Corinthians 10:1–13; Luke 13:1–9

Wade in the Water

Wade in the water,
Wade in the water, children,
Wade in the water,
God's a-gonna trouble the water.

See that band all dressed in white
God's a-gonna trouble the water.
The leader looks like an Israelite.
God's a-gonna trouble the water.

See that band all dressed in red
God's a-gonna trouble the water.
It looks like the band that Moses led.
God's a-gonna trouble the water.
          —*Songs of Zion*, 129

The image of water is prominent in many Spirituals. Waters, like the Jordan River, had to be crossed to reach freedom. In the Middle Passage from Africa to the Western world, the enslaved were carried on ships on the oceans, the waters, to a destination not of their choosing. On the trip, some chose to jump into the waters and drown because death was better than life. Waters can be viewed as a death but also life. We see what water can do through a hurricane's impact. We see what watery fluids can do in a mother's womb as a baby is born. The waters of baptism are a dying and rising for the new believer. There are many meanings of water.

This classic spiritual is about the children of Israel approaching the Red Sea and needing it to be parted because they need to cross over to escape Pharaoh's army. They were the band of people Moses led, and it encourages them to take the risk to "wade in the water . . . [because] God's a-gonna trouble the water." The emphasis of hope is on that latter phrase because in the song, it is the community that sings that part—"God's a-gonna trouble the water." It's louder and stronger. It is the statement of faith. The water may represent trouble, but God is going to trouble their trouble! God is going to trouble your trouble! That is real double trouble. Wade in the water. Take the risk to move forward even without full knowledge of what is to come or how it is to come because God's a-gonna trouble your water.

> Ho, everyone who thirsts,
>   come to the waters;
> and you that have no money,
>   come, buy and eat!
> Come, buy wine and milk
>   without money and without price.
>   (Isa. 55:1)

Prayer for the Day
God, trouble my trouble today. Thank you.

Day 4 (Thursday)

Psalm 31:9–16; Isaiah 53:10–12; Hebrews 2:1–9

I'm Troubled in Mind

Refrain:
I'm troubled, I'm troubled, I'm troubled in mind;
And if Jesus don't help me, I surely will die.

When through the deep waters of trouble I go,
The billows of sorrow cannot overflow.

I'm troubled, etc.

Oh, come here, my Jesus, and help me along,
Till up in bright glory, I sing a new song.

I'm troubled, etc.
*—Folk Song of the American Negro**

* John Wesley Work, *Folk Song of the American Negro* (Nashville: Fisk University Press, 1915), 51.

One of the ways humans experience trouble is in their minds. "I'm troubled in mind." How relevant this is in our day as we see and hear about mental health issues. These issues occur for a wide variety of reasons. There's not just one reason but many. Regardless of the reason, what we know is that mental health issues are on the rise, especially among college-age students. And of course, medicine and religion can work together to make people whole again. We can't pray these issues away nor can we medicate our problems away. But what is certain is that "if Jesus don't help me, I surely will die." That is a theological proclamation!

Jesus is essential to our survival. Jesus can help us find mental equilibrium. Again, it doesn't mean that one cannot and should not be aided by medicine, if and when necessary. But let's face it, Jesus is the *real* Doctor! Whatever mental anguish may be occurring in your life or in others you know, know that Jesus wants you and them to live and not die. "Come here, my Jesus, and help me along." Let that be your prayer this day.

> Be gracious to me, O Lord, for I am in distress;
>   my eye wastes away from grief,
>   my soul and body also.
> For my life is spent with sorrow,
>   and my years with sighing;
> my strength fails because of my misery,
>   and my bones waste away.
>   . . .
> But I trust in you, O Lord;
>   I say, "You are my God."
> My times are in your hand;
>   deliver me from the hand of my enemies and
>   persecutors.

Let your face shine upon your servant;
save me in your steadfast love.
                (Ps. 31:9–10, 14–16)

Prayer for the Day
Jesus, help!

Day 5 (Friday)

Psalm 39; Ezekiel 17:1–10; Romans 2:12–16

City Called Heaven

I am a poor pilgrim of sorrow,
I'm tossed in this wide world alone,
No hope have I for tomorrow,
I've started to make heav'n my home.

Sometimes I am tossed and driven, Lord,
Sometimes I don't know where to roam,
I've heard of a city called heaven,
I've started to make it my home.

My mother has reached that pure glory,
My father's still walkin' in sin,
My brothers and sisters won't own me,
Because I am tryin' to get in.

Sometimes I am tossed and driven, Lord,
Sometimes I don't know where to roam,
I've heard of a city called heaven,
I've started to make it my home.

—*Songs of Zion*, 135

This spiritual reveals that sometimes what is happening on earth leads one to yearn for heaven. Earth is so tough that it isn't home; therefore, heaven becomes a home, a yearned-for home. It is true that some, or even many, feel "tossed in this wide world alone, no hope have [they] for tomorrow." This is a fact of life. Life can be full of lament, and as Christians we should be honest about this, especially during Lent! And the truth be told, the expression of lament is a doxological posture before God. You can lament before God and God can handle it—our questions, our cries, our anger. The Spirituals are like the psalms in that way.

There is truth and honesty in this spiritual. Sometimes we do feel like pilgrims of sorrow, tossed and driven, don't know where to roam. Today, be honest with God about your journey. Express yourself fully and totally and know that what we experience here does not exhaust our experience with God. Our earthly cities may struggle but there is a city where Jesus is the light. Trust that your eternal home is waiting for you no matter what you may be going through. Tell God what's on your heart because God is your real home.

When Gentiles, who do not possess the law, do instinctively what the law requires, these, though not having the law, are a law to themselves. They show that what the law requires is written on their hearts, to which their own conscience also bears witness; and their conflicting thoughts will accuse or perhaps excuse them on the day when, according to my gospel, God, through Jesus Christ, will judge the secret thoughts of all.

(Rom. 2:14–16)

Prayer for the Day

I don't know where to roam. Take me home to your presence, for you are my home.

Day 6 (Saturday)

Numbers 13:17–27; Psalm 39; Luke 13:18–21

God Got Plenty O' Room

God got plenty o' room, got plenty o' room,
'Way in de kingdom,
God got plenty o' room my Jesus say,
'Way in de kingdom.

Brethren, I have come again,
'Way in de kingdom,
To help you all to pray and sing,
'Way in de kingdom.

So many-a weeks and days have passed
Since we met together last.

Old Satan tremble when he sees
The weakest saints upon their knees.

Prayer makes the darkest cloud withdraw,
Prayer climbed the ladder Jacob saw.

Daniel's wisdom may I know,
Stephen's faith and spirit sure.

John's divine communion feel,
Joseph's meek and Joshua's zeal.

There is a school on earth begun
Supported by the Holy One.

We soon shall lay our school-books by,
And shout salvation as I fly.
                              —*Slave Songs*, 128

God got plenty o' room. God makes space for us " 'way in de kingdom," and God makes space for us in his heart. God got plenty o' room in himself. This spacious heart of God calls us to prayer. It doesn't matter if you are a "super Christian" or an "almost Christian" (John Wesley), God has made room for you and your prayers. The weakest saints can pray. Offer a prayer because "prayer makes the darkest cloud withdraw, prayer climbed the ladder Jacob saw." Wisdom, faith, spirit, communion, meekness, zeal? What do you need? What do you desire?

Prayer is "a school on earth begun supported by the Holy One." In this school, you sit in the classroom of the Spirit who leads you into the heart of God. May you learn all of the lessons in the school of prayer you need on this day.

He said therefore, "What is the kingdom of God like? And to what should I compare it? It is like a mustard seed that someone took and sowed in the garden; it grew and became a tree, and the birds of the air made nests in its branches."

And again he said, "To what should I compare the kingdom of God? It is like yeast that a woman took and mixed in with three measures of flour until all of it was leavened."

(Luke 13:18–21)

Prayer for the Day
Thank you, O God, for making room for me in your kingdom.

Week Five

Day 1 (Monday)

Joshua 4:1–13; Psalm 32; 2 Corinthians 4:16–5:5

Almost Over

Some seek de Lord and they don't seek him right,
Pray all day and sleep all night;

Refrain:
And I'll thank God, almost over, almost over, almost over,
    (My Lord)
And I'll thank God, almost over.

Sister, if your heart is warm,
Snow and ice will do you no harm.

I been down, and I done been tried,
I been through the water, and I been baptized.

O sister, you must mind how you step on the cross,
Your foot might slip, and your soul get lost.

And when you get to heaven, you'll be able for to tell
How you shunned the gates of hell.

Wrestle with Satan and wrestle with sin,
Stepped over hell and come back agin.

Slave Songs, 97

"Some seek de Lord and they don't seek him right." How do you seek God? Do you seek God, rightly? We can approach God and do so out of the wrong motivations. We may be asking for the wrong things or things that may hurt us. We may be asking him out of selfish motives. Our approach to God may be only about us and our needs and our wants. We ought to check ourselves before we wreck ourselves!

"O sister, you must mind how you step on the cross, your foot might slip, and your soul get lost." Again, how we seek God or treat God is mentioned in this verse. Some may step on the cross, disrespect what it means for the Christian faith or just overlook it and view it as unimportant. Some may just focus on the empty tomb and resurrection and step right all over the crucifixion. Yet, there is no resurrection without the crucifixion. We shouldn't step on the cross but "lift high the cross." Honor it because of who is on it—Jesus the Christ. Stepping on it, as a Christian, means stepping on Jesus. No wonder our soul would get lost if we did this. So be careful how you seek God and how you treat Jesus. It is "almost over," but let's be sure you "git over" to the other side. Ask God to search your heart, clean it, and cause you to seek him in the right way.

So we do not lose heart. Even though our outer nature is wasting away, our inner nature is being renewed day by day. For this slight momentary affliction is preparing us for an eternal weight of glory beyond all measure, because we look not at what can be seen but at what cannot be seen; for what can be seen is temporary, but what cannot be seen is eternal.

(2 Cor. 4:16–18)

Prayer for the Day

In my seeking of You, O God, let me find salvation and let me find restoration for my soul.

Day 2 (Tuesday)

Joshua 4:14–24; Psalm 32; 2 Corinthians 5:6–15

I Stood on de Ribber ob Jerdon

I stood on de ribber ob Jerdon,
to see dat ship come sailin' ober;
stood on de ribber ob Jerdon,
to see dat ship sail by.

Refrain:
O moaner, don' ya weep,
when ya see dat ship come sailin' ober
Shout "Glory Hallelujah!"
When ya see dat ship sail by.

O sister, ya bettuh be ready
To see dat ship come sailin' ober;
Brother, ya bettuh be ready
To see dat ship sail by.

O preacher, ya bettuh be ready
To see dat ship come sailin' ober;

80

Deacon, ya bettuh be ready
To see dat ship sail by.
—*Songs of Zion*, 149

Many Spirituals talk about the Jordan River and water in general. Boats, ships are also a part of these stories many times. In this story, the ship that is sailin' ober is carrying people to the other side of the river, to heaven, to their eternal home. This is why the singer tells us to "shout 'Glory, Hallelujah!'" One day, we all will be on that ship sailing ober, and ya bettuh be ready. This journey is the grand equalizer—it will include sisters, moaners, preachers, and everyone.

Wherever we are standing right now, even if it's the ribber ob Jerdon or Jordan Lake in Durham, North Carolina, be ready, get ready. One day, the ship will come to us to bring us over. Right now, it may just be sailing by, but soon it will sail directly to you. Will you be ready for this trip? How will you prepare?

The LORD said to Joshua, "Command the priests who bear the ark of the covenant, to come up out of the Jordan." Joshua therefore commanded the priests, "Come up out of the Jordan." When the priests bearing the ark of the covenant of the LORD came up from the middle of the Jordan, and the soles of the priests' feet touched dry ground, the waters of the Jordan returned to their place and overflowed all its banks, as before.
(Josh. 4:15–18)

Prayer for the Day

I want to be ready to sail to you.

Day 3 (Wednesday)

Exodus 32:7–14; Psalm 32; Luke 15:1–10

Lord, Remember Me

Oh Deat' he is a little man,
And he goes from do' to do',
He kill some souls and he wounded some,
And he lef' some souls to pray.

Refrain:
Oh Lord, remember me,
Do, Lord, remember me;
Remember me as de year roll round,
Lord, remember me.

I want to die like-a Jesus die,
And he die wid a free good will,
I lay out in de grave and I stretchee out e arms,
Do, Lord, remember me.

—*Slave Songs*, 15

We may have memory problems at times. Forgetting some things, remembering some things, even selectively.

We might remember wrongly or rightly. Birthdays, people's names, phone numbers, events—all of these things we may struggle to remember. The Bible, itself, is a memory book of the work of God throughout history. Jesus even told his disciples, "Do this in remembrance of me" (1 Cor. 11:24).

Yet it's not always the case that we are called to remember. God also remembers. "Do Lord, remember me." There's nothing wrong with asking God to do this. Remember me. Don't forget about me and my situation. "Remember me as de year roll round." Remember me today, now, and forever. Ask the Lord to remember. He's ready.

> But Moses implored the LORD his God, and said, "O LORD, why does your wrath burn hot against your people, whom you brought out of the land of Egypt with great power and with a mighty hand? Why should the Egyptians say, 'It was with evil intent that he brought them out to kill them in the mountains, and to consume them from the face of the earth'? Turn from your fierce wrath; change your mind and do not bring disaster on your people. Remember Abraham, Isaac, and Israel, your servants, how you swore to them by your own self, saying to them, 'I will multiply your descendants like the stars of heaven, and all this land that I have promised I will give to your descendants, and they shall inherit it forever.'" And the LORD changed his mind about the disaster that he planned to bring on his people.
>
> (Exod. 32:11–14)

Prayer for the Day

Jesus, remember me, when you come into your kingdom.

Day 4 (Thursday)

Joshua 5:9–12; Psalm 32; 2 Corinthians 5:16–21;
Luke 15:1–3, 11b–32

Don't Be Weary, Traveller

Don't be weary, traveller,
Come along home to Jesus;
Don't be weary, traveller,
Come along home to Jesus.

My head got wet with the midnight dew,
Come along home to Jesus;
Angels bear me witness too,
Come along home to Jesus.

Where to go I did not know
Ever since he freed my soul.

I look at de worl' and de worl' look new,
I look at de worl' and de worl' look new.
—*Slave Songs*, 75

Sometimes we get weary. Weary from well-doing. Weary
from work. Weary from studying. Weary from daily

workouts. Weary from climbing up the rough side of the mountain. As travelers on the earth, we get weary. The singer would not have to say, "Don't be weary," if this wasn't the case. He knew we, humans, get weary. Even youth grow tired and get weary (Isa. 40:30). All ages, all sizes, all hues, all denominations, all faiths can get weary because this is a part of being human, even as a Christian.

The question becomes, however, what do you do when you get weary? Where do you turn? To whom do you turn? The singer stresses, "Come along home to Jesus." Jesus says, "Come to me, all you that are weary and are carrying heavy burdens, and I will give you rest" (Matt. 11:28). Rest for your souls. Rest for your body. Rest for your heart. Jesus is our ultimate home. Look no further today, as Jesus is waiting for you with open arms. Come home.

> From now on, therefore, we regard no one from a human point of view; even though we once knew Christ from a human point of view, we know him no longer in that way. So if anyone is in Christ, there is a new creation: everything old has passed away; see, everything has become new! All this is from God, who reconciled us to himself through Christ, and has given us the ministry of reconciliation; that is, in Christ God was reconciling the world to himself, not counting their trespasses against them, and entrusting the message of reconciliation to us.
>
> (2 Cor. 5:16–19)

Prayer for the Day
I am weary and worn. Please give me rest.

Day 5 (Friday)

Leviticus 23:26–41; Psalm 53; Revelation 19:1–8

Oh, Wretched Man That I Am

Refrain:
Oh, wretched man that I am;
Oh, wretched man that I am;
Oh, wretched man that I am;
Who will deliver poor me?

I'm bowed down with a burden of woe,
I'm bowed down with a burden of woe,
I'm bowed down with a burden of woe,
Who will deliver poor me?

Oh, wretched man that I am, etc.

My heart's filled with sadness and pain,
My heart's filled with sadness and pain,
My heart's filled with sadness and pain,
Who will deliver poor me?

—*Folk Song of the American
Negro* (1915), 53

Lent is a liturgical season of sorrow and penitence. It is a time for introspection and reflection as we prepare for the cross and open tomb. It is a time, if there is a time, to be brutally honest about oneself and one's state in life. This spiritual pushes us to be honest about where we might find ourselves in life. There's no shame to acknowledge "my heart's filled with sadness and pain." We don't have to avoid this true expression of our hearts. God wants the truth from us, about us. Sometimes you might even say, "I'm bowed down with a burden of woe," or "Oh, wretched man that I am." There's nothing wrong with these statements in the life of faith.

The Spirituals move us toward honest faith and truthfulness and lament. There can be no hope if we aren't truthful. This is raw and real. Let yourself be real today. In God's holy presence, we are all wretched and we need God to deliver us. Who will deliver poor us? God will. You can count on it!

> Fools say in their hearts, "There is no God."
>> They are corrupt, they commit abominable acts;
>> there is no one who does good.
>
> God looks down from heaven on humankind
>> to see if there are any who are wise,
>> who seek after God.
>
> They have all fallen away, they are all alike
>>> perverse;
>> there is no one who does good,
>> no, not one.
>
> (Ps. 53:1–3)

Prayer for the Day

I am a wretched person in your presence. Deliver me that I might be free.

Day 6 (Saturday)

Leviticus 25:1–19; Psalm 53; Revelation 19:9–10

Tryin' to Get Home

Lord, I'm bearin' heavy burdens,
Tryin' to get home;
Lord, I'm bearin' heavy burdens,
Tryin' to get home;
Lord, I'm bearin' heavy burdens,
Lord, I'm bearin' heavy burdens,
Lord, I'm bearin' heavy burdens,
Tryin' to get home.

Lord, I'm climbin' high mountains,
Tryin' to get home;
Lord, I'm climbin' high mountains,
Tryin' to get home;
Lord, I'm climbin' high mountains,
Lord, I'm climbin' high mountains,
Lord, I'm climbin' high mountains,
Tryin' to get home.

Lord, I'm standin' hard trials,
Tryin' to get home;

> Lord, I'm standin' hard trials,
> Tryin' to get home;
> Lord, I'm standin' hard trials,
> Lord, I'm standin' hard trials,
> Lord, I'm standin' hard trials,
> Tryin' to get home.
>
> —*Songs of Zion*, 130

Many of the Spirituals yearn for "home." This is because the enslaved were stripped from their home and many of their family ties, pulled apart from mother, father, brother, and sister. The family was torn apart, thus home for them was demolished. Literally then, they were "tryin' to get home." This was not just a desire to get home to heaven. Where and what is home for you?

The enslaved didn't have a choice about their separation from home. It was forced dislocation. It is no wonder then that the singer repeats, "I'm bearin' heavy burdens" or "I'm climbin' high mountains" or "I'm standin' hard trials." These are definitely songs of sorrow. A great emphasis is on this tone and expression, a kind of blues sensibility. Some Christians may not be comfortable with this because it's not praise but lament or because they think a life of faith is only about being "happy clappy." The Spirituals help us not to forget the bitter sorrow that is also important to discipleship and give us permission to name it openly. Spirituals open the book of lament. I hope you will read it to learn how this can also lead you to God.

> The Lord spoke to Moses on Mount Sinai, saying: Speak to the people of Israel and say to them: When you enter the land that I am giving you, the land shall observe a sabbath for the Lord. For six years you shall sow your field, and for six years you shall prune your

vineyard, and gather in their yield; but in the seventh year there shall be a sabbath of complete rest for the land, a sabbath for the LORD: you shall not sow your field or prune your vineyard. You shall not reap the aftergrowth of your harvest or gather the grapes of your unpruned vine: it shall be a year of complete rest for the land. You may eat what the land yields during its sabbath—you, your male and female slaves, your hired and your bound laborers who live with you; for your livestock also, and for the wild animals in your land all its yield shall be for food.

(Lev. 25:1–7)

Prayer for the Day

Take me home, Jesus.

Week Six

Day 1 (Monday)

2 Kings 4:1–7; Psalm 53; Luke 9:10–17

You Hear the Lambs a-Cryin'

Refrain:
You hear the lambs a-cryin',
hear the lambs a cryin',
hear the lambs a-cryin',
O Shepherd, feed my sheep.
You feed my sheep.

Leader: My Savior spoke these words so sweet,
Response: O Shepherd, feed my sheep,
Leader: sayin', "Peter, if you love me, feed my sheep."
Response: O Shepherd, feed my sheep.

Leader: Lord, I love Thee, Thou dost know;
Response: O Shepherd, feed my sheep.
Leader: O give me grace to love Thee more.
Response: O Shepherd, feed my sheep.

Leader: Wasn't that an awful shame?
Response: O Shepherd, feed my sheep.

Leader: He hung three hours in mortal pain.
Response: O Shepherd, feed my sheep.
                              —*Songs of Zion,* 128

The lambs are cryin'. People are dying. Youth are crying. Do you hear it? We might say, "O Shepherd, feed my sheep." As this spiritual repeats that line, it is the right thing to say because it recognizes who the Shepherd is. At the same time, we hear, "You feed my sheep," and Jesus says, "Peter, if you love me, feed my sheep." Jesus doesn't leave us off the hook. There is a call to discipleship and partnership with God. There is one Shepherd, but the Shepherd urges us to feed his sheep.

The lambs are cryin', but you have a role to play in feeding them and meeting their need as well. There is a call to action or mission. The Shepherd feeds us, and we can feed others and co-labor with God in holy service. The lambs are cryin' because they are hungry and thirsty. Will you feed them or let them die?

The day was drawing to a close, and the twelve came to him and said, "Send the crowd away, so that they may go into the surrounding villages and countryside, to lodge and get provisions; for we are here in a deserted place." But he said to them, "You give them something to eat." They said, "We have no more than five loaves and two fish—unless we are to go and buy food for all these people." For there were about five thousand men. And he said to his disciples, "Make them sit down in groups of about fifty each." They did so and made them all sit down. And taking the five loaves and the two fish, he looked up to heaven, and blessed and broke them, and gave them to the disciples to set before the crowd. And all ate and were filled. What was left over was gathered up, twelve baskets of broken pieces.

(Luke 9:12–17)

Prayer for the Day
O Shepherd, feed my sheep.

Day 2 (Tuesday)

Psalm 126; Isaiah 43:1–7; Philippians 2:19–24

De Blin' Man Stood on de Road an' Cried

O, de blin' man stood on de road an' cried.
O, de blin' man stood on de road an' cried.

Cryin' O, my Lord, save-a me,
De blin' man stood on de road an' cried.

Cryin' dat he might receib his sight.
Cryin' dat he might receib his sight.

Cryin' O, my Lord, save-a me,
De blin' man stood on de road an' cried.

Cryin' what kind o' shoes am dose you wear,
Cryin' what kind o' shoes am dose you wear.

Cryin' O, my Lord, save-a me,
De blin' man stood on de road an' cried.

Cryin' dese shoes I wear am de Gospel shoes,
Cryin' dese shoes I wear am de Gospel shoes.

Cryin' O, my Lord, save-a me,
De blin' man stood on de road an' cried.
—*Books of American Negro Spirituals*, 108–9

This spiritual about the blind man is based on Luke 18 (cf. Mark 10). In the Bible, the blind man is healed, but in this spiritual, there is no healing. Only a cry and lots of it. Crying, crying, and more crying. The blind man stood on the road and cried. That's it. No resolution to a problem. That's how it is sometimes. Sometimes, there's only a cry to be heard, and that's okay. We don't have to rush to a solution or resolution. The crying is authentic and it is a crying out to God: "O, my Lord, save-a me."

Some Christians aren't comfortable with crying, but Spirituals were not created to make anyone comfortable. They were a matter of survival. The cry may actually be a source of freedom, to give voice to your pain like nothing else can, to cry out to God freely. This blind man is an example of how to do that. Learn from him today and cry out.

Restore our fortunes, O Lᴏʀᴅ,
    like the watercourses in the Negeb.
May those who sow in tears
    reap with shouts of joy.
Those who go out weeping,
    bearing the seed for sowing,
shall come home with shouts of joy,
    carrying their sheaves.

(Ps. 126:4–6)

Prayer for the Day

I cry out for your hand of mercy to heal me. O, my Lord, save me.

Day 3 (Wednesday)

Psalm 126; Isaiah 43:8–15; Philippians 2:25—3:1

Steal Away

Refrain
Steal away, steal away, steal away to Jesus!
Steal away, steal away home, I ain't got long to stay here!

My Lord calls me,
He calls me by the thunder;
The trumpet sounds within-a my soul,
I ain't got long to stay here.

Green trees are bending,
Poor sinner stands a-trembling;
The trumpet sounds within-a my soul,
I ain't got long to stay here.

Tombstones are bursting,
Poor sinner stands a-trembling;
The trumpet sounds within-a my soul,
I ain't got long to stay here.

My Lord calls me,
He calls me by the lightning,
The trumpet sounds within-a my soul,
I ain't got long to stay here.

—*Songs of Zion*, 134

I ain't got long to stay here! How true that is! Every second we march closer to our death. And though the days may seem long, the years feel short. We don't have that long on earth, really. That is sobering, yet true. We may want to go to Jesus now. We might want to steal away to Jesus, to go to heaven, to reach home. What's interesting about this spiritual in particular is although it can be read as an otherworldly spiritual, it is also a classic example of the double meaning or "mask" of many Spirituals.

This spiritual also had to do with this world. Steal away, steal away could have also meant "let's get away" to freedom up north to Canada and been used as code messages to the enslaved about attempting to escape. "I ain't got long to stay here" takes on two meanings then. Either way, it suggests that where you are now is not where you will be forever. Life isn't stagnant in God. There is always movement. Whatever it is, wherever it is, be ready to steal away when God says it's time.

Before me no god was formed,
    nor shall there be any after me.
I, I am the LORD,
    and besides me there is no savior.
I declared and saved and proclaimed,
    when there was no strange god among you;
    and you are my witnesses, says the LORD.

I am God, and also henceforth I am He;
 there is no one who can deliver from my hand;
 I work and who can hinder it?

(Isa. 43:10b–15)

Prayer for the Day
*Lord, I know I don't have long to stay here. Call me when you
are ready.*

Day 4 (Thursday)

Exodus 12:21–27; Psalm 126; John 11:45–57

Soon-a-Will Be Done-a-with Troubles of the World

Refrain:
Soon-a-will be done-a-with the troubles of the world,
Troubles of the World;
Soon-a-will be done-a-with the troubles of the world,
Goin' home to live with God.

These are my Father's children,
These are my Father's children,
These are my Father's children,
All in-a-one band.

Soon-a-will be done-a-with the troubles of the world, etc.

No more weeping and-awailing,
No more weeping and-awailing,
No more weeping and-awailing,
All in-a-one band.

Soon-a-will be done-a-with the troubles of the world, etc.
—*Folk Song* (1915), 56

103

This is one of my favorite Spirituals. Soon-a will be done-a with the troubles of the world. I've sung it all over the world at churches and universities. It is a portable song that expresses a human experience. There are troubles in the world without a doubt, but soon we'll be done with them. Troubles cannot terrorize us forever. They will not. It takes courage to say that.

This spiritual is courageous as it names the trouble. No more weeping and a-wailing. The singer declares enough is enough! All the pain. Enough! All the weeping. Enough! All the wailing. Enough! All the trouble. Enough! Let this song be your song this day. No more trouble because I'm "goin' home to live with God." Remember, trouble don't last always!

So from that day on they planned to put him to death. Jesus therefore no longer walked about openly among the Jews, but went from there to a town called Ephraim in the region near the wilderness; and he remained there with the disciples.

(John 11:53–54)

Prayer for the Day

Show me, Jesus, that trouble doesn't last always. Touch my heart to know that my troubles will soon be over, for you have overcome them.

Day 5 (Friday)

Isaiah 43:16–21; Psalm 126;
Philippians 3:4b–14; John 12:1–8

Go Down, Moses

When Israel was in Egypt's land: Let my people go;
Oppressed so hard they could not stand, Let my people go.

Go down, Moses, 'Way down in Egypt land,
Tell ole Pharaoh, Let my people go.

"Thus said the Lord," bold Moses said, Let my people go;
"If not, I'll smite your first-born dead," Let my people go.

Go down, Moses, 'Way down in Egypt land,
Tell ole Pharaoh, Let my people go.

No more shall they in bondage toil, . . .
Let them come out with Egypt's spoil, . . .

When Israel out of Egypt came, . . .
And left the proud oppressive land, . . .

O, 'twas a dark and dismal night, . . .
When Moses led the Israelites, . . .

'Twas good old Moses and Aaron, too, . . .
'Twas they that led the armies through, . . .

The Lord told Moses what to do, . . .
To lead the children of Israel through, . . .

O come along, Moses, you'll not get lost, . . .
Stretch out your rod and come across, . . .

As Israel stood by the water side, . . .
At the command of God it did divide, . . .

When they had reached the other shore, . . .
They sang the song of triumph o'er, . . .

Pharaoh said he would go across, . . .
But Pharaoh and his host were lost, . . .

Oh, Moses, the cloud shall clear the way, . . .
A fire by night, a shade by day, . . .

You'll not get lost in the wilderness, . . .
With a lighted candle in your breast, . . .

Jordan shall stand up like a wall, . . .
And the walls of Jericho shall fall, . . .

Your foes shall not before you stand, . . .
And you'll possess fair Canaan's land, . . .

'Twas just about in harvest-time, . . .
When Joshua led his host divine, . . .

Oh, let us all from bondage flee . . .
And let us all in Christ be free, . . .

We need not always weep and moan, . . .
And wear these slavery chains forlorn, . . .

　　　　　　　　　　—Songs of Zion, 112

This classic spiritual depicts the biblical story about
the exodus of the children of Israel out of Egypt led by
Moses. This spiritual has been a metaphor for the experience of African Americans during the time of slavery.
Pharaoh was the White slave master. Israel represented
the enslaved Blacks. Egypt was the United States. Moses
was anyone who was leading the people to freedom. It is a
song that represents a double meaning. The people sang
this not only to retell the biblical story but to tell their
story toward freedom.

All throughout this spiritual, "let my people go" is
repeated. It is the voice of God speaking to Pharaoh.
Musically, this line is sung by the entire community. The
community is the voice of God in this spiritual, revealing
that sometimes what we hear from others is God speaking to us. God uses others to speak to us. "Let my people
go." I wonder what you might have to let go of today or
what needs to let go of you. What is holding you hostage?
Why aren't you free? You are not alone. A community of
support and faith is telling whatever is entrapping you—
"let my people go." Be free!

Thus says the LORD,
　　who makes a way in the sea,
　　a path in the mighty waters,
who brings out chariot and horse,
　　army and warrior;
they lie down, they cannot rise,
　　they are extinguished, quenched like a wick:

Do not remember the former things,
    or consider the things of old.
I am about to do a new thing;
    now it springs forth, do you not perceive it?
I will make a way in the wilderness
    and rivers in the desert.
The wild animals will honor me,
    the jackals and the ostriches;
for I give water in the wilderness,
    rivers in the desert,
to give drink to my chosen people,
    the people whom I formed for myself
so that they might declare my praise.

                         (Isa. 43:16–21)

Prayer for the Day

Go down, Jesus. Way down in my life. And set me free.

Day 6 (Saturday)

Exodus 40:1–15; Psalm 20; Hebrews 10:19–25

I Want Jesus to Walk with Me

I want Jesus to walk with me;
I want Jesus to walk with me;
All along my pilgrim journey, Lord,
I want Jesus to walk with me.

In my trials, Lord, walk with me;
In my trials, Lord, walk with me;
When my heart is almost breaking, Lord,
I want Jesus to walk with me.

When I'm in trouble, Lord, walk with me;
When I'm in trouble, to walk with me;
When my head is bowed in sorrow, Lord,
I want Jesus to walk with me.
—*Songs of Zion*, 95

No one wants to walk the road of life alone. No one. We all want company. We all want *com-panis* ("with bread"). We all want to be "with bread," to have sustenance on the journey. No wonder this spiritual declares, "I want Jesus to walk with me." Jesus is our daily bread, the bread of life. He is our true companion on the way. Notice that whether in trials or in trouble, when hearts are breaking, or heads are bowed in sorrow, the plea is not to remove the trials or trouble, the plea is for Jesus to "walk with me." Just his presence is enough because to be with him is to be with God. And at the end of the day, that's what everyone wants—to be with God, to know that Jesus is Immanuel, "God with us" (Matt 1:23). Wherever you travel this day, may you know deep companionship with Christ, who will never leave you nor forsake you. Walk on.

> Now I know that the LORD will help his anointed;
>> he will answer him from his holy heaven
>> with mighty victories by his right hand.
> Some take pride in chariots, and some in horses,
>> but our pride is in the name of the LORD our God.
> They will collapse and fall,
>> but we shall rise and stand upright.

(Ps. 20:6–8)

Prayer for the Day
With everything I'm going through, Jesus, walk with me, please.

Holy Week

Day 1 (Monday)

Judges 9:7–15; Psalm 20; 1 John 2:18–28

Nobody Knows the Trouble I've Had

Nobody knows de trouble I've had,*
Nobody knows but Jesus,
Nobody knows de trouble I've had,
Glory hallelu!

One morning I was a-walking down, O yes, Lord!
I saw some berries a-hanging down, O yes, Lord!
O yes, Lord I saw some berries hanging down.

I pick de berry and I suck de juice, O yes, Lord!
Just as sweet as the honey in de comb, O yes, Lord!

Sometimes I'm up, sometimes I'm down,
Sometimes I'm almost on de groun'.

What make ole Satan hate me so?
Because he got me once and he let me go.

*I see.

—*Slave Songs*, 74

This is another classic Spiritual that speaks the truth! We need the truth and nothing but the truth. "Sometimes I'm up, sometimes I'm down, Sometimes I'm almost on de groun'." Up and down, up and down. This can be life. This can be your life even as a Christian. Of course, there are times when we get to enjoy the juice from a berry and honey in de comb. But what this spiritual reveals is how often "nobody knows de trouble I've had." That line is repeated and is part of the refrain of this spiritual. Trouble, trouble, trouble.

Yet, like the movement of lament psalms, this spiritual doesn't close out with trouble. Rather, it rings out with a word of hope and praise. "Glory hallelu!" Glory hallelu? This singer knows something about God. Something happens between all of the trouble and this trumpet-tongued praise at the end. This slave singer knows that our trouble will not terrorize us forever. This singer knows that hope will have the final word. This singer knows God will win and triumph over all of our trouble! As Jesus said, "In this world you will have trouble. But take heart! I have overcome the world" (John 16:33 NIV). Yes, you may be experiencing trouble but in the midst of that, you can still say, "Glory hallelu," because even if you make your bed in Sheol, God is there (Ps. 139). This should make anyone declare, "Glory hallelu!"

> When it was told to Jotham, he went and stood on the top of Mount Gerizim, and cried aloud and said to them, "Listen to me, you lords of Shechem, so that God may listen to you.
>
>> The trees once went out
>>   to anoint a king over themselves.
>> So they said to the olive tree,
>>   'Reign over us.'

The olive tree answered them,
    'Shall I stop producing my rich oil
    by which gods and mortals are honored,
    and go to sway over the trees?'
Then the trees said to the fig tree,
    'You come and reign over us.'
But the fig tree answered them,
    'Shall I stop producing my sweetness
    and my delicious fruit,
    and go to sway over the trees?'
Then the trees said to the vine,
    'You come and reign over us.'
But the vine said to them,
    'Shall I stop producing my wine
    that cheers gods and mortals,
    and go to sway over the trees?'
So all the trees said to the bramble,
    'You come and reign over us.'
And the bramble said to the trees,
    'If in good faith you are anointing me king over
      you,
    then come and take refuge in my shade;
    but if not, let fire come out of the bramble
and devour the cedars of Lebanon.'"

                    (Judg. 9:7–15)

Prayer for the Day
God, I don't ask for anything. I just have one thing to say—
glory hallelu!

Day 2 (Tuesday)

Leviticus 23:1–8; Psalm 31:9–16; Luke 22:1–13

We Shall Overcome

We shall overcome,
We shall overcome,
We shall overcome someday.
Oh, if in our hearts we do believe,
We shall overcome someday.

We'll walk hand in hand . . .

We shall all have peace . . .

We are not afraid . . .

God is on our side . . .
—*Songs of Zion*, 127

What makes an impression on my heart when engaging the Spirituals is their dogged faith in God. And from that deep sense of faith, hope rises. The Lenten journey has been long and it can even be exhausting. There have been challenges. There have been trials. There have been ups and downs. Valleys, lonesome valleys, dangerous valleys, vicious valleys. Yet despite the fright of the dark nights of the soul, somehow, someday, we can say, "We shall overcome." We shall all have peace. We are not afraid. Why? I believe there are two reasons.

First, there is a *we* not *me*. We are not alone on this journey. We have companionship and a community on the way. I find it interesting that it's not "I" shall overcome but "we" shall overcome. I can't really overcome without you overcoming. It is a collective victory. Second, and most important, we don't have to be afraid because "God is on our side." The presence of God brings assurance and hope that we shall overcome someday. This wasn't new for the leaders of the civil rights movement in the United States of the 1960s; this faith was rooted in the deep spirituality of the enslaved and continues to breathe today. Remember, the life of faith includes "we," and the "we" is how God wants it to be on the journey. Don't forget those who helped you overcome and those who need you to help them overcome. And most of all, don't forget the God who brings us all out in victory!

Now the festival of Unleavened Bread, which is called the Passover, was near. The chief priests and the scribes were looking for a way to put Jesus to death, for they were afraid of the people.

Then Satan entered into Judas called Iscariot, who was one of the twelve; he went away and conferred with the chief priests and officers of the temple police about how he might betray him to them. They were greatly pleased and agreed to give him money. So he

consented and began to look for an opportunity to
betray him to them when no crowd was present.

(Luke 22:1–6)

Prayer for the Day

*God, lead us to be on your side so that we shall overcome, not
just someday, but every day.*

Day 3 (Wednesday)

Psalm 51; Isaiah 30:15–18; Hebrews 4:1–13

Fix Me, Jesus

Refrain:
Oh, fix me; Oh, fix me;
Oh, fix me; fix me, Jesus, fix me.

Fix me for my long, white robe;
Fix me, Jesus, fix me.
Fix me for my starry crown;
Fix me, Jesus, fix me.

Fix me for my journey home;
Fix me, Jesus, fix me.
Fix me for my dying bed.
Fix me, Jesus, fix me.
—*Songs of Zion*, 122

Computers need fixing. Cars need fixing. Doors need fixing. We don't normally hear, "We need fixing." We can travel throughout life, going about our daily routine, without any thought about our need. We go to work.

We come home. We eat. We sleep. And then the next morning we start all over again, and perhaps without any mind of how we are doing. I didn't say what we are doing, but *how*. In assessing our lives, honestly, we will realize that we need fixing too. Everything is not always right with us—emotionally, spiritually, mentally, physically, relationally.

This simple spiritual tells it all—fix me. Not "fix him" or "fix her" or "fix them" or "fix us." Fix me. It's me who needs help. It's me who needs fixing. It's personal. What in your life needs fixing? Jesus is the faithful fixer. Ask him to fix you. May you have eyes to see where you need fixing.

> Have mercy on me, O God,
>   according to your steadfast love;
> according to your abundant mercy
>   blot out my transgressions.
> Wash me thoroughly from my iniquity,
>   and cleanse me from my sin.
>   (Ps. 51:1–2)

Prayer for the Day
Fix me, Jesus, fix me.

Day 4 (Holy Thursday)

Isaiah 52:13–53:12; Psalm 22; Hebrews 4:14–16; 5:7–9

Calvary

Refrain:
Calvary, Calvary,
Calvary, Calvary,
Calvary, Calvary,
Surely he died on Calvary.

Ev'ry time I think about Jesus,
Ev'ry time I think about Jesus,
Ev'ry time I think about Jesus,
Surely he died on Calvary. [Refrain]

Don't you hear the hammer ringing?
Don't you hear the hammer ringing?
Don't you hear the hammer ringing?
Surely he died on Calvary. [Refrain]

Don't you hear him calling his Father?
Don't you hear him calling his Father?
Don't you hear him calling his Father?
Surely he died on Calvary. [Refrain]

Don't you hear Him say, "It is finished"?
Don't you hear Him say, "It is finished"?
Don't you hear Him say, "It is finished"?
Surely he died on Calvary. [Refrain]

Jesus furnished my salvation.
Jesus furnished my salvation.
Jesus furnished my salvation.
Surely he died on Calvary. [Refrain]

Sinner, do you love my Jesus?
Sinner, do you love my Jesus?
Sinner, do you love my Jesus?
Surely he died on Calvary. [Refrain]
                              —*Songs of Zion*, 87

There are times in life when one word will suffice to capture a mood or event. Too many words wouldn't do it justice. One word is sufficient. Words like love or peace or joy. And then to say the word only once would be insufficient; it has to repeated to mirror its scope and impact. Love, love, love, love. Peace, peace, peace, peace. Joy, joy, joy, joy. By doing so, we amplify its essence. In all of these, the repetition signifies the surplus that is inherent in them. Love spills over on to others. Peace is to be shared. Joy is to the world!

In the same way, "Calvary" captures the essential image and location of the death of Jesus. Surely he died on Calvary. That word said once would point to this. But this word repeated amplifies it and presents the wideness of its impact on the world. Calvary, Calvary, Calvary. It's unavoidable. Calvary, the place of Christ's death. Surely he died on Calvary. You can't avoid it or escape it. He died. Accept it. Accept the cross of Calvary and the callous heart of humanity that crucified him. The hammer rang and he died. Sit with that. Don't ignore Calvary. Calvary is calling you and it's asking you, "Do you love my Jesus?" Do you?

> Since, then, we have a great high priest who has passed through the heavens, Jesus, the Son of God, let us hold fast to our confession. For we do not have a high priest who is unable to sympathize with our weaknesses, but we have one who in every respect has been tested as we are, yet without sin. Let us therefore approach the throne of grace with boldness, so that we may receive mercy and find grace to help in time of need. . . . In the days of his flesh, Jesus offered up prayers and supplications, with loud cries and tears, to the one who was able to save him from death, and he was heard because of his reverent submission. Although he was a Son, he learned obedience through what he suffered; and having been made perfect, he became the source of eternal salvation for all who obey him.
>
> (Hebrews 4:14–16; 5:7–9)

Prayer for the Day
Jesus Christ, you died that I might live. You said, "It is finished," but you are not finished with me.

Day 5 (Good Friday)

Psalm 31:9–16; Isaiah 54:9–10; Hebrews 2:10–18

Were You There?

Were you there when they crucified my Lord? (were you
    there?)
Were you there when they crucified my Lord? Oh!
Sometimes it causes me to tremble, tremble, tremble.
Were you there when they crucified my Lord?

Were you there when they nailed Him to the tree? (to the
    tree?)
Were you there when they nailed Him to the tree? Oh!
Sometimes it causes me to tremble, tremble, tremble.
Were you there when they nailed Him to the tree?

Were you there when they pierced Him in the side? (in
    the side?)
Were you there when they pierced Him in the side? Oh!
Sometimes it causes me to tremble, tremble, tremble.
Were you there when they pierced Him in the side?

Were you there when the sun refused to shine? (were you
    there?)

Were you there when the sun refused to shine? Oh!
Sometimes it causes me to tremble, tremble, tremble.
Were you there when the sun refused to shine?

Were you there when they laid Him in the tomb? (in the
  tomb?)
Were you there when they laid Him in the tomb? Oh!
Sometimes it causes me to tremble, tremble, tremble.
Were you there when they laid Him in the tomb?
                                    —*Songs of Zion*, 126

Were you there? We were not there, historically. But this
spiritual takes us there, to the place of grotesque suffering
and the death of the Christ. They crucified him. Nailed
him. Pierced him. The sun refused to shine because the
Light of the world was murdered and laid in a tomb, dead.
It should make us tremble, tremble, tremble, if we sit with
it, if we ponder it, if we allow ourselves to go there.

I realize some don't like to go there. They want a
bleached Christ who has no blood, no pain, no misery.
They want a triumphant Christ without a cross, but the
wounds of the crucifixion will not be erased by the resurrection. This is the truth. And it should make us tremble—
that the religious and civic leaders killed God in Christ and
at that moment it looked like the Savior needed to be saved.

Ponder what all of this means to you. Don't shy away
from the cross. Go there and view his bruised and blood-
ied body. Go there and see God hanging from a tree. Go
there and learn from this suffering God. Go there and
tremble. Tremble before this terror. Tremble before the
One who was torn apart for you. Tremble at this kind of
cruciform love. Were you there? I hope you will go there.

Since, therefore, the children share flesh and blood,
he himself likewise shared the same things, so that

through death he might destroy the one who has the power of death, that is, the devil, and free those who all their lives were held in slavery by the fear of death. For it is clear that he did not come to help angels, but the descendants of Abraham. Therefore he had to become like his brothers and sisters in every respect, so that he might be a merciful and faithful high priest in the service of God, to make a sacrifice of atonement for the sins of the people. Because he himself was tested by what he suffered, he is able to help those who are being tested.

(Heb. 2:14–18)

Prayer for the Day

Without the sun shining, without your light, today, I tremble because I am there at the foot of the cross.

Day 6 (Holy Saturday)

Psalm 39; Jeremiah 11:1–17; Romans 2:1–11

He Never Said a Mumbalin' Word

They crucified my Lord,
and he never said a mumbalin' word;
they crucified my Lord,
and he never said a mumbalin' word.
Not a word, not a word, not a word.

They nailed him to a tree,
and he never said a mumbalin' word;
they nailed him to a tree,
and he never said a mumbalin' word.
Not a word, not a word, not a word.

They pierced him in the side,
and he never said a mumbalin' word;
they pierced him in the side,
and he never said a mumbalin' word.
Not a word, not a word, not a word.

The blood came trickalin' down,
and he never said a mumbalin' word;

> the blood came trickalin' down,
> and he never said a mumbalin' word.
> Not a word, not a word, not a word.
>
> He bowed his head and died,
> and he never said a mumbalin' word;
> he bowed his head and died,
> and he never said a mumbalin' word.
> Not a word, not a word, not a word.
> —*Songs of Zion*, 101

Silence can be underrated. In today's culture, words seem to win the day. Words on TV, words in magazines, words on Twitter or Facebook, words on blogs, the war of words. Who is the loudest with words is often heard, but in the pause and space between the words, there is the break, the silence. It is often overlooked and not heard, yet there is the music of silence. Words come out of silence and return to silence. If there was only noise, we wouldn't know what silence was nor could we distinguish it from noise or words. Sometimes, we need to be silent.

Jesus demonstrates this at such a tragic time. He's being crucified, nailed to a tree, pierced in his side, blood trickalin' down, and he eventually died. He could have said a lot of things to his oppressors, but "he never said a mumbalin' word." Never. "Like a sheep that before its shearers is silent, so he did not open his mouth" (Isaiah 53:7b). Not a word, not a word, not a word. Sometimes not saying a word is the best thing to say; words can be weapons, and as the saying goes, silence can be golden. Jesus was just present to the moment. He didn't say anything with his mouth but said it all with his body. "This is my body, which is given for you" (Luke 22:19). That's what was said in the silence. You could see the Word speaking this without saying any word whatsoever. Sometimes, we may underestimate the role of silence in the spiritual life, but it can be constructive and helpful and the most appropriate response. It was for Jesus. How about you?

> I said, "I will guard my ways
>> that I may not sin with my tongue;
> I will keep a muzzle on my mouth
>> as long as the wicked are in my presence."
> I was silent and still;
>> I held my peace to no avail;
> my distress grew worse,
>> my heart became hot within me.
> While I mused, the fire burned;
>> then I spoke with my tongue:
>
> "LORD, let me know my end,
>> and what is the measure of my days;
>> let me know how fleeting my life is.
>
> "And now, O Lord, what do I wait for?
>> My hope is in you.
> Deliver me from all my transgressions.
>> Do not make me the scorn of the fool.
> I am silent; I do not open my mouth,
>> for it is you who have done it."
>
> (Ps. 39:1–4, 7–9)

Prayer for the Day

Word of God, help me to know when to speak and when not to say a word.

CPSIA information can be obtained
at www.ICGtesting.com
Printed in the USA
FSHW022142020419
56907FS